First published in 2011 by
MACMILLAN EDUCATION AUSTRALIA PTY LTD
15–19 Claremont Street, South Yarra 3141

Visit our website at www.macmillan.com.au or go directly to www.macmillanlibrary.com.au

Associated companies and representatives throughout the world.

National Library of Australia Cataloguing-in-Publication entry

Pyers, Greg.
    Of grasslands / Greg Pyers.
    ISBN: 9781420278880 (hbk.)
    Biodiversity.
    Includes index.
    For primary school age.
    Grassland ecology—Australia—Juvenile literature.

577.40994

Publisher: Carmel Heron
Commissioning Editor: Niki Horin
Managing Editor: Vanessa Lanaway
Editor: Georgina Garner
Proofreader: Tim Clarke
Designer: Kerri Wilson
Page layout: Raul Diche
Photo researcher: Wendy Duncan (management: Debbie Gallagher)
Illustrator: Richard Morden
Production Controller: Vanessa Johnson

Printed in China

Acknowledgements
The author and publisher are grateful to the following for permission to reproduce copyright material:

Front cover photograph: Bison grazing in Theodore Roosevelt National Park, North Dakota courtesy of
Ardea/Tom & Pat Leeson.
Back cover photographs courtesy of Shutterstock/Four Oaks (elephant); Shutterstock/Rina Lyubavina (everlasting flower).

Photographs courtesy of:
Corbis/John Carnemolla, **18**, /Gallo Images/Hein Von Horsten, **17**, /Mike Grandmaison, **27**, Blaine Harrington III, **20**, /Peter
Johnson, **4**; Getty Images/Discovery Channel Images/Jeff Foott, **19**; istockphoto/Joerg Thsymm, **10**; photolibrary/Alamy/Dave
and Sigrun Tollerton, **9**, /OSF/Mark MacEwen, **24**, /OSF/Stan Osolinski, **13**, /Photo Researchers/Mark Boulton, **21**, /Jeff
Vanuga, **29**; Shutterstock/Ewan Chesser, **25**, /EcoPrint, **7**, /Eric Isselée, **22**, /LightShaper, **28**, /Christopher Meder Photography,
16, /Nestor Noci, **15**, /Bernhard Richter, **23**. Background and design images used throughout courtesy of Shutterstock/Rina
Lyubavina (flower), /Iakov (grass).

While every care has been taken to trace and acknowledge copyright, the publisher tenders their apologies for any accidental
infringement where copyright has proved untraceable. They would be pleased to come to a suitable arrangement with the
rightful owner in each case.

Please note
At the time of printing, the Internet addresses appearing in this book were correct. Owing to the dynamic nature of the
Internet, however, we cannot guarantee that all these addresses will remain correct.

Contents

Glossary words

When a word is printed in **bold**, you can look up its meaning in the Glossary on page 31.

What is biodiversity?

Biodiversity, or biological diversity, describes the variety of living things in a particular place, in a particular **ecosystem** or across the whole Earth.

Measuring biodiversity

The biodiversity of a particular area is measured on three levels:

- **species** diversity, which is the number and variety of species in the area
- genetic diversity, which is the variety of **genes** each species has. Genes determine the characteristics of different living things. A variety of genes within a species enables it to **adapt** to changes in its environment.
- ecosystem diversity, which is the variety of **habitats** in the area. A diverse ecosystem has many habitats within it.

Egrets, buffaloes and grass plants are part of the biodiversity of some African grasslands.

Species diversity

Some habitats, such as coral reefs and rainforests, have very high biodiversity. One scientific study found 534 species in 5 square metres of coral reef in the Caribbean Sea. In the Amazon Rainforest, in South America, 50 species of ants and many other species were found in just 1 square metre of leaf litter. In desert habitats, the same area might be home to as few as ten species.

Habitats and ecosystems

Grasslands are habitats, which are places where plants and animals live. Within a grassland habitat, there are also many smaller habitats, sometimes called microhabitats. Some grassland microhabitats are tussock grass clumps, the undersides of rocks and the soil. Different kinds of **organisms** live in these places. The animals, plants, other living things and non-living things and all the ways they affect each other make up a grassland ecosystem.

Biodiversity under threat

The variety of species on Earth is under threat. There are somewhere between 5 million and 30 million species on Earth. Most of these species are very small and hard to find, so only about 1.75 million species have been have been described and named. These are called known species.

Scientists estimate that as many as 50 species become **extinct** every day. Extinction is a natural process, but human activities have sped up the rate of extinction by up to 1000 times.

Known species of organisms on Earth

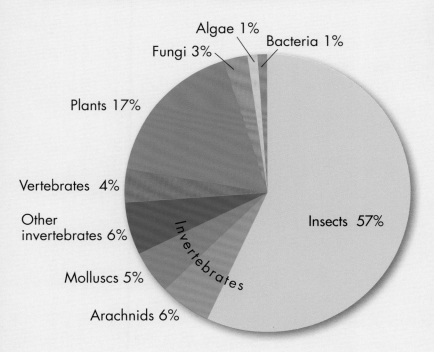

- Algae 1%
- Bacteria 1%
- Fungi 3%
- Plants 17%
- Vertebrates 4%
- Other invertebrates 6%
- Molluscs 5%
- Arachnids 6%
- Insects 57%
- Invertebrates

The known species of organisms on Earth can be divided into bacteria, algae, fungi, plant and animal species. Animal species are classified as vertebrates or invertebrates.

Approximate numbers of known vertebrate species

ANIMAL GROUP	KNOWN SPECIES
Fish	31 000
Birds	10 000
Reptiles	8 800
Amphibians	6 500
Mammals	5 500

Why is biodiversity important?

Biodiversity is important for many reasons. The diverse **organisms** in an **ecosystem** take part in natural processes essential to the survival of all living things. Biodiversity produces food and medicine. It is also important to people's quality of life.

Natural processes

Humans are part of many ecosystems. Our survival depends on the natural processes that go on in these ecosystems. Through natural processes, air and water are cleaned, waste is decomposed, **nutrients** are recycled and disease is kept under control. Natural processes depend on the organisms that live in the soil, on the plants that produce oxygen and absorb **carbon dioxide**, and on the organisms that break down dead plants and animals. When **species** of organisms become **extinct**, natural processes may stop working.

Food

We depend on biodiversity for our food. The world's major food plants are grains, vegetables and fruits. These plants have all been bred from plants in the wild. Wild plants are important sources of **genes** for breeding new disease-resistant crops. If these plants become extinct, their genes are lost.

Medicine

About 40 per cent of all prescription drugs come from chemicals that have been extracted from plants. Scientists discover new, useful plant chemicals every year. The United States National Cancer Institute discovered that 70 per cent of plants found to have anti-cancer properties were rainforest plants. When plant species become extinct, the chemicals within them are lost forever.

Did you know?

Wheat is a wild grass that is native to the region between eastern Turkey and Jordan. People have grown wheat for food for about 10 000 years. It is one of the world's most important food crops.

Quality of life

Biodiversity is important to people's quality of life. Animals and plants inspire wonder. They are part of our **heritage**. The animals of the eastern African grasslands, such as lions, cheetahs, elephants, rhinoceroses and zebras, are among the best known of all species. They are powerful symbols of the importance of grassland biodiversity.

The African lion is an important symbol of bravery and strength to people all over the world. Lions are one example of how biodiversity inspires wonder and awe and this improves our quality of life.

Extinct species

The quagga was an unusual type of zebra that lived on the dry grasslands of South Africa. The head and front part of its body was striped, but the rest of its body was one brown colour. Humans hunted the quagga for its meat and its hide, and to stop it from grazing in farmed areas. The last wild quagga was shot by hunters in the 1870s, and the last known quagga died in a zoo in Amsterdam in 1883.

Grasslands of the world

Grasslands are open areas where the dominant plants are grasses. Many other small plants grow among the grasses, too. There are grasslands on all continents except Antarctica.

Where grasslands are found

Grasslands usually grow in areas that have too little rainfall to support trees, but too much rainfall to form deserts, or where it is too cold for trees to grow. Grasslands can be found in **tropical** areas, in alpine areas and along coasts. Grasslands may cover very large areas or they may be in small pockets among other **habitats**, such as forests and woodlands.

This map shows the major grassland areas mentioned in this book.

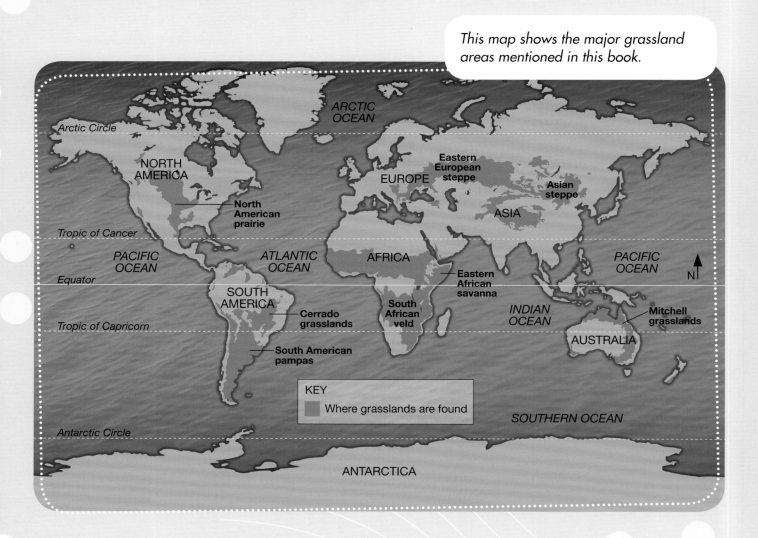

ARCTIC OCEAN

Arctic Circle

NORTH AMERICA

EUROPE

Eastern European steppe

Asian steppe

ASIA

North American prairie

Tropic of Cancer

PACIFIC OCEAN

ATLANTIC OCEAN

AFRICA

PACIFIC OCEAN

N

Equator

SOUTH AMERICA

Eastern African savanna

Cerrado grasslands

South African veld

INDIAN OCEAN

Mitchell grasslands

Tropic of Capricorn

AUSTRALIA

South American pampas

KEY

Where grasslands are found

SOUTHERN OCEAN

Antarctic Circle

ANTARCTICA

Los Llanos, in Venezuela and Colombia, are tropical grasslands that are flooded by rivers each year. More than 700 species of birds are found in these grasslands.

Types of grasslands

Grasslands differ from one another in the types of plant and animal **species** that they contain. These differences are due to many factors, including **climate** and soil type.

Temperate grasslands

Temperate grasslands have a climate of cold winters and hot summers, with rainfall between 500 and 900 millimetres a year. The soil is **fertile** and deep, and there are fires in the hot summer months. There are few or no trees in temperate grasslands. Examples of temperate grasslands are the steppes of eastern Europe and Asia, the veld of South Africa, the pampas of South America and the prairie of North America.

Tropical grasslands

Tropical grasslands have a hot climate, with a few months of heavy rain. They receive 500 to 1300 millimetres of rainfall a year. The habitat is called **savanna** if the trees grow scattered about and in small numbers. Savanna may also be described as woody grassland if it has few trees or as grassy woodland if it has many trees. Examples of tropical grasslands are the Serengeti savanna of eastern Africa and the Mitchell grasslands of northern Australia.

In the dry season, grassland fires encourage new grass to grow and they also kill tree seedlings, which prevents a savanna from becoming a forest. In the wet season, tropical grasslands may have long periods of flooding, which prevents the growth of most trees.

Grassland biodiversity

Each type of grassland has its own level of biodiversity. Soil type and **climate** determine which **species** of grasses and other plants grow in a grassland, and this **vegetation** determines which animal species live there.

Soil types

The soil that is found in **temperate** grasslands is among the most **fertile** soil in the world. This **nutrient**-rich soil was formed over many years as the dense network of grass roots rotted and then grew again. The fertile soil supports the growth of tall and short grass species and many species of **forbs**.

The soil of **tropical** grasslands is not usually as fertile as that of temperate grasslands. It is also usually quite porous, which means that water drains through it quickly.

Climate types

The climate of an area affects which grasses will grow there and how they will grow. Hummock grasslands are found in dry climates. The grasses grow in clumps, and there may be small flowering plants between the clumps or, in dry years, bare soil. Tussock grasslands grow in areas that have more reliable rainfall. The tussocks grow loosely together, with forbs inbetween. Closed grasslands are found in wet areas, such as on floodplains. The grasses grow very close together and there may be no spaces between them.

In this desert grassland in Karijini National Park in Western Australia, hummock grasses grow in clumps.

Grassland plant biodiversity

Grasses are the most obvious grassland plants, but there may be many other plant species in a grassland. In the grasslands of south-eastern Australia, there are more than 700 species of other plants, including orchids, daisies and lilies. Many of these plants grow underground for much of the year and are visible only when they flower in spring and summer.

Grassland animal biodiversity

Temperate grasslands usually have lower animal biodiversity than tropical grasslands. The table below compares the biodiversity of mammals in one type of temperate grassland with the biodiversity of mammals in one type of tropical grassland.

Mammals in a temperate and a tropical grassland

TYPE OF GRASSLAND	TYPE OF MAMMAL	
	HOOFED **HERBIVORE**	CARNIVORE
North American prairie (temperate grassland)	Examples are American bison, pronghorn antelope, deer and elk	Examples are grey wolf, black-footed ferret, coyote, American badger and long-tailed weasel
Eastern African **savanna** (tropical grassland)	More than 40 species, including zebra, wildebeest, buffalo, elephant, warthog, hippopotamus, white rhinoceros and antelope species	Examples are lion, cheetah, jackal, hyena, African wild dog, banded mongoose and small cat species

Termites

Many grasslands are home to tiny, grass-eating termites. Millions of these insects live in large nests, which they build from soil and saliva. At night, the termites travel across the grassland, using tunnels that they have built below the ground. They collect grass and plant remains and bring them back to their nests.

Grassland ecosystems

Living and non-living things, and the **interactions** between them, make up a grassland **ecosystem.** Living things are plants and animals. Non-living things are the rocks, soil, water and **climate**.

Food chains and food webs

A very important way that different **species** interact is by eating or consuming other species. This transfers energy and **nutrients** from one **organism** to another. A food chain illustrates this flow of energy and nutrients by showing what eats what. Food chains are best set out in a diagram. A food web shows how many different food chains fit together.

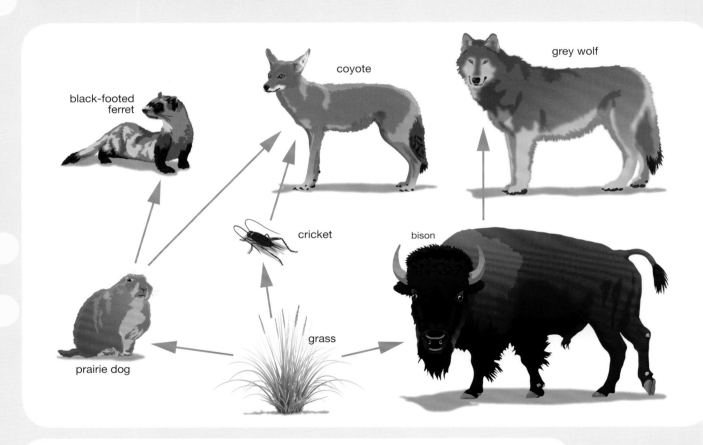

This prairie grassland food web is made up of several food chains. In one food chain, grasses are eaten by prairie dogs, which in turn are eaten by coyotes.

Other interactions

Non-living and living things in a grassland interact in other ways, too. In North American prairies, prairie dogs dig burrows, which allow air into the soil. This is important for healthy grass growth. In the grasslands of south-eastern Australia, striped legless lizards hide from **predators** and shelter from fire in cracks that form in the soil during summer.

Grass growth

Unlike other plants such as trees and shrubs, grasses grow from the base of the plant. When animals graze grass, they eat the top parts of the plants and the bottom growing parts are not eaten. The grazed leaves simply grow back from the base of the plant. These growing parts are also protected from fire.

Fire and grasslands

Fire is important to how a grassland ecosystem works. Fire burns away dead thatches of grass that build up over the year, giving other plants room to grow. Ash from the fire **fertilises** the soil. In **savannas**, fire kills tree seedlings and prevents the growth of forests.

Fire has an effect on biodiversity within a grassland, too. Grazing animals are attracted to recently burned areas, where new shoots are growing. Areas that have not burned in a long time have dense **vegetation** in which small animals can shelter and nest.

Humans sometimes use fire to encourage new growth in grasslands. These fires are often called controlled burns. This controlled burn will mean new grass will grow, providing food for animals such as elephants.

Threats to grasslands

Grasslands are threatened by a range of human activities. Farmers, villagers and **invasive species** move into grasslands and displace and kill native species. **Climate** change is changing grassland **habitats**.

Biodiversity hotspots

There are around 34 regions in the world that have been identified as biodiversity hotspots. The biodiversity of these regions is under severe threat from humans. These hotspots have many **endemic species**. Many of the world's biodiversity hotspots include grasslands.

The Cerrado

The Cerrado is a **tropical** grassland and biodiversity hotspot in Brazil. It is the only biodiversity hotspot that is mostly **savanna**. It contains areas of dense forest and scrubland within the savanna, and rivers flow through the hotspot. The species biodiversity of the Cerrado is very high and many species are endemic.

The Cerrado grasslands cover more than 2 million square kilometres of central Brazil, in South America.

Animal and plant species of the Cerrado	
GROUP	APPROXIMATE NUMBER OF KNOWN SPECIES
Plants	Around 10 000 (4 400 are endemic species)
Reptiles	225 (33 are endemic species)
Amphibians	186 (28 are endemic species)
Mammals	195 (14 are endemic species)
Fish	800 (200 are endemic species)
Birds	607 (17 are endemic species)

Note: This table includes species from all habitats in the Cerrado, including grasslands.

Major threats to the Cerrado

Agriculture is the major threat to the Cerrado. The region is quite flat and has **fertile** soil and good rainfall, which make it very suitable for crops and grazing.

In the 1970s, introduced pastures and crops began to replace native grasses in the Cerrado. Corn, soybean, rice, wheat and eucalyptus were introduced, as well as African pasture grasses for livestock. Trees were logged to make charcoal for the steel industry.

Today, one-quarter of Brazil's crop production comes from the Cerrado region, and 40 million cattle are grazed there. Around 120 000 square kilometres of the Cerrado have been cleared in the past six years, which is a rate twice as fast as the clearing of the Amazon Rainforest. About 20 per cent of the original Cerrado **vegetation** remains.

Did you know?

The maned wolf of the Cerrado has very long legs, giving it a good view of its grassland habitat as it stalks rabbits, mice, birds and lizards. The changing of grasslands to agricultural land in the Cerrado is threatening the maned wolf's survival.

The giant anteater is threatened by habitat loss caused by land clearing in the Cerrado in Brazil.

BIODIVERSITY THREAT: Farming

Grasslands can be very easily converted into farming land, because they are often on flat ground and there are no forests to clear. In many parts of the world, large areas of grassland have been taken over to graze livestock and to grow crops such as wheat.

Grazing

Many grasslands have been destroyed by the grazing of **domestic** cattle, sheep and goats. Introduced animals may eat **forb species** so heavily that many of these common plants become rare or **extinct**.

Where natural grasslands have been eaten, graziers need to plant pastures for their animals. Planted pastures are artificial grasslands. Unlike natural grasslands, they usually consist of just a few introduced plant species and they cannot support high animal biodiversity.

Mongolian–Manchurian grasslands

These **temperate** grasslands cover an area of almost 1 million square kilometres in Mongolia and inland China. Przewalski's gazelles, Przewalski's horses and Bactrian camels once lived there. These animals were overhunted, and graziers brought in sheep and goats in large numbers.

A herdsman grazes goats on the Mongolian–Manchurian grasslands. Domestic goats have eaten many small grassland plants to extinction.

Veld is a grassland of South Africa. Some veld has been lost to cattle-grazing and cropping.

Cropping

Where farmers have cleared grasslands and planted crops, they have often planted just one species of plant in each field. This creates an unbalanced **ecosystem**. Each of the plants in the field needs the same types of **nutrients** from the soil, and the plants can use up all of these particular nutrients. Only some species feed on or live among the planted crop, and their numbers may grow very large. Other species lose their **habitats**.

Pampas grasslands

The Pampas covers 600 000 square kilometres of Argentina. Most of this area was grassland, but in the last few hundred years it has been taken over for crops and grazing. The original grassland **vegetation** exists in small pockets that are too remote or rugged to farm. The Pampas deer is the main **herbivore** of the region, but it is now threatened because of habitat loss and **poaching**.

Traditional land management

For thousands of years, indigenous people such as Indigenous Australians and Native Americans used fire to keep grasslands open and to create a patchwork of vegetation at different stages of growth. Fire encouraged the growth of plants, and with a high diversity of plants, there was a high diversity of animals.

BIODIVERSITY THREAT:
Invasive species

Introduced **species** are non-native species that are introduced into a **habitat**. Some become **invasive species**, which spread widely and take over from native species. They change the grassland **ecosystem**.

Introducing non-native species

Non-native species are introduced into a habitat either accidentally or deliberately. Many invasive plant species escape from farms. Black wattle is a small tree from Australia that was taken to South Africa as a timber and shelter plant. Each plant is able to produce thousands of seeds each year, and the seeds can be carried into grasslands on animals, on car tyres and by water. Black wattle grows thickly, turning grassland into shrubland.

Other species are introduced deliberately. In 1859, European rabbits were released in Australia for hunting. By 1910 they had spread across the country and had a population of up to 800 million. They ate many grassland plant species to **extinction**. Rabbits compete with native animals for food, but they are also prey for some native animals, such as wedge-tailed eagles.

Prairie weeds

In 1896, Chinese bush clover was planted in the United States to provide feed for cattle and to control **erosion**. It has since spread into prairie grasslands, where it displaces native plants.

Rabbits were introduced from Europe to Australia in 1859. They sometimes breed so quickly they reach plague numbers.

Invasive grassland species

Some introduced species thrive because they are free of the diseases that affected them in their place of origin and free of the animals that ate them. Plant species that become invasive are often well **adapted** to growing in areas that have been disturbed by human activities such as road-building. These species may produce seeds that sprout quickly in the disturbed soil along roadsides. They then spread rapidly along roads and into surrounding grasslands.

Mexican poppy

Mexican poppy is an invasive species in Serengeti **savanna** in Tanzania. The poppy first appeared south-west of Ngorongoro Crater, which is a vast grassland with a very high biodiversity of mammals. It is also a **World Heritage Site**. The plants probably grew from seeds that had been accidentally carried in a shipment of wheat seeds.

As Mexican poppy spreads through the savanna, it competes with native grasses, and animals that usually graze on native grasses cannot eat Mexican poppy. Already, some individual plants of Mexican poppy have been found inside Serengeti National Park, which is also a World Heritage Site.

Mexican poppy is an invasive species in the grasslands of Tanzania. It also spreads through farmland, competing with crops.

BIODIVERSITY THREAT:
Conflict with people

Increasing human populations need more space, and towns and cities are spreading out into grasslands. This destroys grassland **habitats**, and in many parts of the world it brings people into conflict with grassland animals.

Kenya's lions and elephants

Kenya's lion population has been decreasing at a rate of about 100 lions a year. Some scientists predict that within 20 years there will be no wild lions at all in Kenya. The main reasons for the fall in lion numbers are due to an increasing human population. When lions move onto private land and kill livestock, farmers respond by poisoning or shooting the lions.

During droughts, when there is little food in the national parks, elephants sometimes wander into farms searching for food. More local people enter the parks to find water for themselves and their livestock. Sometimes the elephants attack the people, so the people kill the elephants.

Tourism

Every year, thousands of tourists visit game reserves to see the **savanna** wildlife of countries such as Tanzania, Kenya and Zimbabwe. Tourism is very important to the economies of these nations. However, tourism must be strictly managed. If there are too many tourists, this can disturb wildlife and affect grassland habitats.

Conflict between humans and wildlife is growing as more tourists and local people visit grassland habitats.

Elephants are hunted for their ivory tusks. Many countries have banned the trade of ivory, but poaching still continues.

Poaching

Poaching is the illegal killing or capture of wild animals to sell for meat, for body parts or as pets. Some people are driven to poaching because they need money and cannot find work. Some people poach animals to provide meat for their families. Other poachers are motivated by greed.

Many grassland animals are threatened by poaching. In Africa, up to 40 000 grassland animals are poached each year for meat and body parts. These body parts include horns and teeth, which are sold to collectors around the world.

Did you know?

In the days of the Roman Empire (about 27 BCE to 395 CE), many African savanna animals were captured and taken to Rome to fight other animals and warriors called gladiators to the death. In one series of battles in 240 CE, 70 lions, 19 giraffes, 30 elephants, ten antelopes, ten hyenas and many more animals were killed, along with 2000 gladiators. So many animals were captured that many **species** disappeared from grassland areas where they once lived.

BIODIVERSITY THREAT:
Climate change

The world's average temperature is rising because levels of certain gases, such as **carbon dioxide**, are increasing in Earth's atmosphere. These gases, called greenhouse gases, trap heat. The increase in temperature is causing **climate** changes that will affect grasslands.

Effects of climate change

Scientists are uncertain how grasslands will be affected by climate change. However, they do know that the amount of rainfall and where it falls will change. In wet grasslands, such as the Cerrado of Brazil, a decline in rainfall might reduce the amount of flooding, which would allow trees to grow and woodland or forest would take over. In other grasslands, there might be an increase in rainfall and temperatures, which would also allow more trees to grow. On the other hand, increased temperatures might increase the frequency and intensity of fires, which kill trees and encourage the growth of grasses.

Climate change is also causing the world's sea level to rise, as polar icecaps melt. As this happens, low-lying coastal grasslands will be flooded.

*If climate change increases rainfall in dry grasslands, more trees might grow and the grasslands might turn into forests. This means grassland animals, such as wildebeest, will lose their **habitats**.*

Climate change in the past

Scientists look to the past to help them make predictions about what might happen to grassland biodiversity as the climate changes. They study fossils to find out how animals **evolved** as the climate changed over millions of years.

Kangaroos and climate change

Fifteen million years ago, rainforest covered most of Australia. Fossils tell us that kangaroos at that time had teeth that were small and best suited to eating fruit and worms, not grass. Their forelegs were only a little shorter than their hindlegs, so they walked rather than hopped. Eight million years ago, Australia began to dry out. Fossils from this time show that kangaroos' hindlegs became much longer than their forelegs. This meant that they hopped, which is a way of moving that is well suited to open country such as grassland. Their teeth were also larger and better suited to eating grass.

Today, the kangaroos of Australia's grasslands have very long hindlegs. Two kangaroo **species** still survive in Australia's rainforests. These animals have long forelegs, which help them climb trees.

As the climate changed over millions of years, most rainforest kangaroo species evolved into the grassland kangaroo species of today.

Grassland conservation

Conservation is the protection, preservation and wise use of resources. Grassland biodiversity needs to be protected from threats caused by human activities. Research, education and the protection of **habitats** and **species** are all part of grassland conservation.

Research

Research surveys and studies are used to find out how grassland **ecosystems** work and how humans affect them. This research helps people work out ways of conserving grasslands. The people who carry out this research are usually scientists employed by governments, universities, botanical gardens, zoos or organisations such as the International Union for Conservation of Nature.

Education

Educating people about grasslands is essential for grassland conservation. If people are shown that grasslands are important as places of beauty, as habitat for many **endemic species** and as a source of **genes** for the breeding of food crops, they will be more likely to help conserve these areas.

A research scientist studies mongooses in the grassland of a national park in Uganda. Through studying grassland animals, scientists can find ways to protect them from human activities.

Habitat conservation

National parks are reserves that have been set aside to protect biodiversity. Many national parks have been established in areas of outstanding natural beauty, such as rainforests and alpine areas. In the past, grasslands were not seen as beautiful places, and people thought of them as open spaces that were best suited to housing or farming. Many large grasslands were lost before their biodiversity was understood and protected. Today, in Africa, the large animals of the grasslands are seen as spectacular and worthy of being protected in national parks.

There may be fewer than 3000 African wild dogs remaining in the wild, so conservation groups are working to protect the species.

Species conservation

Each grassland species faces different threats, and some conservation groups work to protect just one species. Zambia's African Wild Dog Conservation works to protect the African wild dog. This species has become highly endangered because of:

- distemper, which is a disease that comes from **domestic** dogs
- poisoning by farmers who are trying to protect their livestock
- being caught in snares, which **poachers** use to catch animals.

The group studies the dogs in the wild and it has an anti-snaring team that finds and destroys snares. In another conservation project in Tanzania, African wild dogs are vaccinated against distemper to protect them from this disease.

CASE STUDY:
North American prairies

The prairies of North America cover 3.6 million square kilometres. The prairies were once vast grasslands, but since Europeans arrived more than 450 years ago, about 90 per cent of these **habitats** have been converted to farmland, roads and urban settlements.

Biodiversity of the prairies

In the west of the prairie area, rainfall is lowest and the prairie is called shortgrass prairie. Dominant grass **species** include blue grama and buffalo grass. Tallgrass prairie is found in the east, where rainfall is higher and the soil is rich in **nutrients**. Here, species such as Indian grass and big bluestem grow to more than 1.5 metres tall. Wildflowers such as arrowleaf balsamroot, Indian paintbrush and wild blue flax grow among the grasses. Mixtures of tallgrass and shortgrass prairie plants are found in the central region.

Animal species of the prairies

The prairie grasslands once supported enormous herds of American bison. These animals were preyed on by wolves, which followed the herds as they **migrated** north and south each year. Coyotes, elk, pronghorn antelopes and jackrabbits were also common. Small rodents called prairie dogs built 'towns', which are networks of tunnels where prairie dog families live.

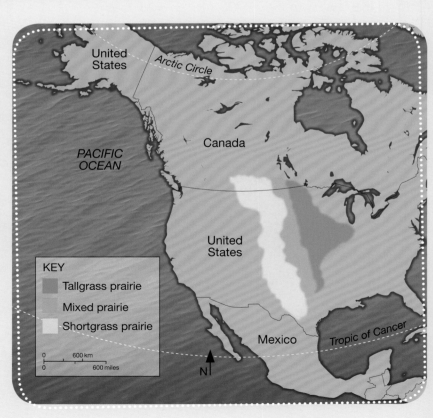

KEY

Tallgrass prairie

Mixed prairie

Shortgrass prairie

0   600 km
0   600 miles

N

The tallgrass, mixed and shortgrass prairies of North America are found in the central United States.

The Grasslands National Park in Canada is an example of mixed prairie grasslands.

Prairie ecosystems

In the past, fire was important to the prairies. It killed tree seedlings and burned away the dense layer of dead grass that built up each year. The ash helped make the soil rich in nutrients. The fresh grass was grazed by millions of bison and other **herbivores**, and their urine and dung enriched the soil.

Humans first arrived on the prairies around 10 000 years ago. They hunted bison for meat and hides, and harvested grassland plants for food.

Disturbing prairie ecosystems

When European settlers arrived, the grassland **ecosystem** quickly changed. In 1862, the United States Government passed a law that allowed settlers to claim 160 acres (about half a square kilometre) of prairie to farm. By 1900, 1 600 000 square kilometres of grassland had been ploughed for crops. Coyotes were shot to protect livestock. Prairie dogs were poisoned and their burrows were ploughed. The burrowing owl, which nests in the prairie dogs' burrows, and the black-footed ferret, which preys on prairie dogs, became rare.

In the grassland areas that remained, fires were put out and not allowed to burn. Bison were shot in huge numbers. Prairie plants that depended on both fire and bison for their survival began to die out.

Prairie conservation

Across the prairie states of the United States, pockets of prairie are being protected. The largest of these areas is the 158-square-kilometre Tallgrass Prairie Preserve in Oklahoma. Fire is used to manage the grasslands in the reserve. About 40 patches, adding up to one-third of the total area, are burned each year. This creates different **habitats** and helps to conserve biodiversity. Cattle farmers in the surrounding areas are being shown how to use fire on their prairies so that they can help with grassland conservation, too. Scientists and students study grassland **ecosystems** at the Tallgrass Prairie Ecological Research Station.

American Prairie Foundation

The American Prairie Foundation is a conservation organisation that works in the state of Montana. Its goal is to preserve and protect private and public prairie land, and to manage the land as a wildlife reserve. It buys prairie land and reintroduces bison to its natural habitat.

In 1994, as part of a conservation effort, 300 bison were reintroduced into the Tallgrass Prairie Preserve in Oklahoma, in the United States. There are now about 2500 in the herd.

The black-footed ferret is still endangered, but its numbers are increasing due to a successful breeding program.

The black-footed ferret

More than 30 years ago, the black-footed ferret was thought to be **extinct**, but a breeding program in the 1980s helped conserve the **species**. The ferret lives in prairie dog burrows, where it shelters and preys on prairie dogs. The ferret population began to fall from the 1860s, when prairie grasslands were taken over for farming. Farmers poisoned prairie dogs to prevent them from digging burrows in their fields, and this destroyed the ferrets' habitat and prey. In 1974 they were thought to be extinct.

In 1981, a farmer's dog caught a black-footed ferret. A search found a colony of 18 ferrets. They were captured so that a breeding colony could be started, safe from poisons and disease. The ferrets bred well.

Since 1991, about 200 ferrets have been released each year into suitable grassland habitats in Mexico, Canada and the United States. In 2009, the wild population was estimated to be about 1000.

Did you know?

It is thought that about 30 million bison once roamed the prairies, but by the 1800s fewer than 1000 remained. Today, due to conservation efforts, there are about 15 000 American bison roaming free and about 500 000 captive bison living on ranches.

What is the future for grasslands?

Grasslands have been under severe threat from human activities for hundreds of years. Grassland biodiversity is falling, but when threats are removed, this decline can be slowed or even stopped. Some **species** may reappear and be saved from **extinction**.

What can you do for grasslands?

You can help protect grasslands in several ways.

- Find out about grasslands. Why are they important and what threatens them?
- If you live in or near a grassland, you can join volunteer groups who replant grassland species on cleared land.
- Become a responsible consumer, and don't litter.
- If you are concerned about grasslands in your area, write to or email your local newspaper, your local member of parliament or another politician and tell them your concerns. Know what you want to say, set out your argument, be sure of your facts and ask for a reply.

Useful websites

🖥 **http://www.blackfootedferret.org**
This website gives information about the black-footed ferret, including ferret facts and information about ferret conservation.

🖥 **http://www.biodiversityhotspots.org**
This website has information about the richest and most threatened areas of biodiversity on Earth.

🖥 **http://www.iucnredlist.org**
The IUCN Red List has information about threatened plant and animal species.

Glossary

adapt   change in order to survive

carbon dioxide   a colourless and odourless gas produced by plants and animals

climate   the weather conditions in a certain region over a long period of time

domestic   tame and kept or cultivated by humans

ecosystem   the living and non-living things in a certain area and the interactions between them

endemic species   species found only in a particular area

erosion   wearing away of soil and rock by wind or water

evolved   changed over time

extinct   having no living members

fertile   capable of producing lots of vegetation, possibly due to a high nutrient content

forb   small flowering plant that grows among grass plants

gene   segment of deoxyribonucleic acid (DNA) in the cells of a living thing, which determines its characteristics

habitat   place where animals, plants or other living things live

herbivore   plant-eating animal

heritage   things we inherit and pass on to following generations

interaction   action that is taken together or actions that affect each other

invasive species   non-native species that spread through habitats

migrate   move from one place to another, especially seasonally

nutrient   chemical that is used by living things for growth

organism   animal, plant or other living thing

poach   illegally hunt or capture wildlife

predator   animal that kills and eats other animals

savanna   very open woodland with grass between the trees

species   a group of animals, plants or other living things that share the same characteristics and can breed with one another

temperate   in a region or climate that has mild temperatures

tropical   in the hot and humid region between the Tropic of Cancer and the Tropic of Capricorn

vegetation   plants

World Heritage Site   a site that is recognised as having great international importance and that is protected by the United Nations Educational, Scientific and Cultural Organization (UNESCO)

Index

A

African wild dogs   11, 25
anteaters   15

B

biodiversity hotspots   14, 30
bison   11, 12, 26, 27, 28, 29
black-footed ferret   11, 12, 27, 29, 30

C

carbon dioxide   6, 22
Cerrado grasslands   8, 14, 15, 22
climate change   14, 22–3
conservation   24–5, 28, 29, 30
coyotes   11, 12, 26, 27
cropping   6, 15, 16, 17, 19, 24, 27

E

ecosystem diversity   4, 6–7, 12–13
ecosystems   4, 6, 12–13, 17, 18, 24, 27, 28
education   24
elephants   20, 21
endangered species   25, 29
endemic species   14, 24
extinct species   5, 6, 7, 16, 18, 29, 30

F

farming   7, 14, 16–17, 18, 19, 20, 25, 26, 27, 28, 29
fire   9, 13, 17, 22, 27, 28
food   6, 21, 24, 27
food chains   12
food webs   12
forbs   10, 16

G

genetic diversity   4, 6, 24
grazing   7, 13, 15, 16, 17, 19, 27

H

habitats   4, 8, 9, 14, 15, 17, 18, 20, 22, 24, 25, 26, 28, 29

I

invasive species   14, 18–19

K

kangaroos   23

L

lions   7, 11, 20, 21

M

medicines   6
Mexican poppy   19
microhabitats   4
Mongolian–Manchurian grasslands   16

P

pampas grasslands   8, 9, 17
poaching   15, 17, 21, 25
prairie dogs   12, 13, 26, 27, 29
prairies   8, 9, 11, 12, 13, 18, 25, 26–9

Q

quagga   7

R

rabbits   15, 18, 26
research   24

S

savannas   8, 9, 11, 13, 14, 15, 19, 20, 21
species diversity   4, 5, 6, 7, 9, 10, 11, 14, 15, 21, 24, 25, 26

T

temperate grasslands   9, 10, 11, 16
termites   11
threats to biodiversity   5, 14–15, 16–17, 18–19, 20–21, 22–3, 30
tropical grasslands   9, 10, 11, 14

W

websites   30
wolves   11, 12, 15, 26